Baby Brain

Kripa PM

BookLeaf
Publishing

India | USA | UK

Presentation by *BookLeaf Publishing*

Web: www.bookleafpub.com

E-mail: info@bookleafpub.com

ISBN: 9789360949624

First edition 2024

This book is dedicated to

Every beautiful human being who is willing to help oneself and everyone around them who are suffering from any kind of mental illness..

with a lot of love..

Your friend - Kripa

ACKNOWLEDGEMENT

Thank you God!!!

Thank you mom and dad, My Therapists, Bangtan, all life coaches, friends and whom ever was there for me always.

I would like to specially thank my better half Ajith who stood with me always with a lot of love and support.

PREFACE

It took 10 years for me to address my mental health issue properly. I did it alone. Courageously. Alone.

Ten years back I have gone through a frightful and unbelievable event for the first time, it lasted for nearly a month. I was just 18. I didn't had a job, I was doing my graduation.

My parents knew that I was going through some hard times but still I was not taken to a psychologist. But they took me to a normal physician as most of the parents do. This might be due to the social stigma and the fear to address the actual issue.

Every hard time was normalised as just fear. But for me it was like a near-death experience that I never wanted to face. I faced it a lot of times but not regularly. I even had thoughts about ending my life so I don't have to face these uninvited horrible sensations that choke me but no one can understand its severity.

I started to learn more about mental health just to keep myself strong.

The more I knew, my fear became less. Even after confronting my struggles with mental health, my own family neglected it at the beginning. They judged me as an overthinker and I'm stuck in a bubble. But later they tried to understand when I started opening up.

I am an MBA graduate and a HR professional. I'm not someone who wishes to live in a bubble. Or someone who dwells on past pains. It was hard to explain anyone that it's not a choice. It's a disease that should be treated with care and support.

Panic attacks, anxiety, PTSD, everything are just fancy words for people who don't know anything about mental health and illness.

In their eyes I might be weak but people who know about these mental disorders know how much strength it will take to get over it one time.

I myself had to find a therapist. It was hard at the beginning but it truly helped me. I kept myself engaged, I did meditation. I had a few friends who were not judgemental and who could understand it. Life was not hard as before after I got few people who listened to me and supported me. Of course, my parents too supported me.

I wanted to write this book for the strongest warriors who fought similar kinds of hard battles alone.

You don't have to do it alone. When you open up few may judge you and question your pain. That's natural because for them it's new or these pains never exist.. But believe me, there are a lot of people who can understand you or help you out. You may feel that you are alone, but you are not.

I wish to say that you are heard, you are not weak and you can cure it with professional help and other techniques.

I have written my thoughts on mental health and self-love. I have tried to express my emotions and thoughts as small poems so that it will reach people as an awareness or a reminder that you can heal your innerchild.

I wanted everyone to check out within your friend circle or family who has gone through such mental illness. You don't have to be a doctor or therapist to help someone. You just have to be someone who really cares. You just have to be a Human.

There are things that are not visible but still we believe. Just like the air you breathe and the God you trust and pray.

I wanted to let everyone understand that mind matters, mental health is as important as physical health. To understand that you have to listen to the person who is trying to tell his/her pain.

Seeking help is not attention-seeking.
Be kind and accept that people can go through stuff you don't know about.

Apology

Hey!! I am Sorry for speaking out
This melancholy is a
malady now.

I know I have to step out
As the cure costs your supremacy somehow.

They said this is LIFE But I'm just burned out
Even if you say It was ordinary,
NO..it's Not..I vow.

We are never the same so please Don't lash out
My pain is true Solemnly
So please don't dismiss it now!

Bye

Bidding goodbye is
Burdensome
But a single bye can bring you peace in
abundance

Like a mid-summer
Blossom
Muggy Life feels light after
Brushing off all the unasked opinions

Let's say goodbye to
The naysayers
And make space for
The comrades

Trust me there are
Believers
They may not be your best buddies but the
Nomads

Confront

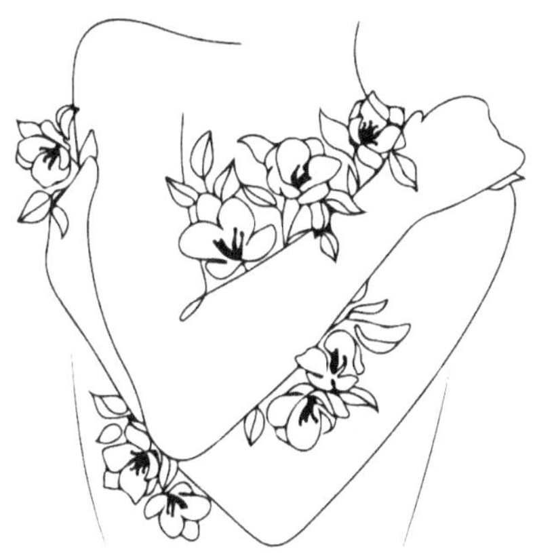

Please Don't burry your painful conflicts
It will be peaceful only for a
fleeting moment

It will come out as deep-rooted sprouts
Eventually you will see a
dark forest

Confront your struggles
unresolved issues will never allow
your mind to take rest

Even if your mind ignores
For peace
Your body will score - As a disease

Denial

Screamed my lungs out of panic
'Cause I heard the most demonic roar
I was just five and it was so tragic
Seeing my world collapsed indoor

Escaping from the evil a million times quitely
Hiding my pain to protect my loved ones
I missed to live my life slowly
As I was between survival and judgements

I buried the pain under my smile
A kid who wanted to live in a home
Never knew that she would be the dustpile
Unseen and unheard even in pain, left all alone

They wanted to save the monster
So they denied her existence
They said the bright light is darker
By choosing an option called avoidance

Equanimity

Unlearning rage
as it is a cage
It is strange
that It is so hard to change
From teenage
there was a poise shortage
So now I exchange the outrage
With a change by weaving verses on a page

Four ways

My Noodles boiled a lot so young
So the new kid in the block
Muddled the memories

Then my baby almond's alarm started
malfunctioning among
The hippo's shrinkage

Sometimes they push me to FIGHT MODE
Telling me to be alert..
Even if I don't want to
My teeth grind n jaw tightens, my body makes
me ready to fight
Before someone starts it

Sometimes they push me to FLIGHT MODE
Telling me to be alert..
Even if I don't want to

My body feels numb and becomes restless, it
makes me ready to escape and run from the
danger

Sometimes they push me to FREEZE MODE
Telling me to be alert
Even if I don't want to
My heart beats slow or fast and I feel stuck, my
body makes me freeze to escape from danger

Sometimes they push me to FAWN MODE
Telling me to be alert
Even if I don't want to
I will tolerate a lot, people please and never say
No,
My body wants me to be safe by being good
always.

These are the trauma responses that show up
often
Even if I don't want to respond
I blamed my brain for making me sick
But now I pamper them a lot 'cause they've
always tried to save me with these tricks

*Almond - Amygdala (looks like almond), the new kid -
prefrontal cortex (youngest organ), Hippo- Hippocampus,
Noodle - Brain. For someone who experienced chronic
trauma or multiple traumas, the Amygdala, PFC and
Hippocampus change their functioning as a result

Amygdala becomes hyperreactive; the PFC size shrinks leading to loss of the ability to distinguish past and present; the Hippocampus shrinkage releases excess cortisol or stress hormones. This is the reason for PTSD and panic attacks. The dysfunction of these brain parts brings the memories again and again as flashbacks and panic attacks; even if you don't want to react, your mind or body will respond to it as if the real traumatic event is still happening!

Generosity

Never stop being good
Even if you were badly screwed

But,

To be good
is not to be tolerant to the rude

To be good
is not to be a doormat to the self-absorbed

To be good
Is not to be a yes man to the wicked

To be good
Is not to be liked by everyone in the world

Generosity doesn't have to visit
Places filled with bad-deeds

Hiraeth

I belong to the nature
My life belongs to the cosmos

I wish I was not tamed
I just wish I was not named

Rather than being a clone
I just wish to be someone unknown

My soul is stuck inside
But it feels like why it should even hide

In search of home
I wandered alone

It was not seen anywhere outside
So I went deep inside

Closed eyes showed me a lot
More than my opened eyes caught

Longing for love
Makes us a home

For the one who needs
We are the home it seems!!!

Invincible

Days are darker
but I'm the light

Nights are longer
but I'm Alright

Even if it's worster
I'll hold me tight

Even if there is a monster
I'll make him quite

Just for misogynists

We won't cover up the problems you created
For saving your reputation!

We won't cover up our bodies you wanted
For controlling your temptation!

We won't cover up our wounds you painted
For giving you the power of domination!

We won't cover up our dreams you denied
For fitting into the box you made of condition!

We won't cover up the flaws you hid
To survive as a woman who is just an attraction!

We won't coverup pain like our mothers you
praised
To reconcile with this Man-made world of
misconception!

Keeper

Love is sweet, love is bitter
Love is high, love is low
Love is joy, love is pain
Love is strength, love is weakness
Love is bright, love is dark
Love is you, love is me
Who loved your lights?
Who loved your shadows?

Light

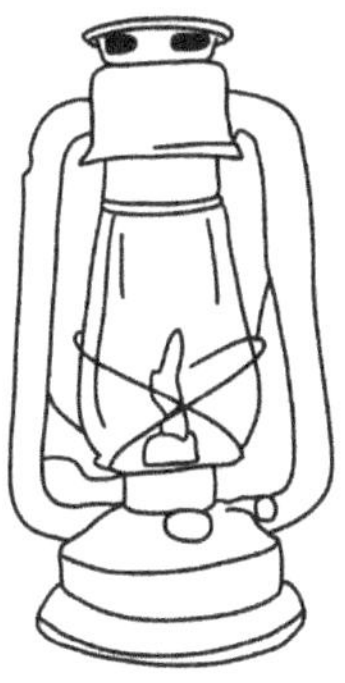

Sometimes you have to
Cross the most darkest time in your life alone...

You may feel helpless and seek help from others
like a crazy clown...

But they may not see
The darkness as it is inside you and it is
unknown

In such times be your own light and believe that
You are your savior with a powerful crown

Let your light absorb the darkness within you
But first.. it's okay to break down!

May be it's me

Is it my disruptive thinking
Or my dysfunctional family

Is it my never-ending nightmares
Or my dysregulated nervous system

Is it my intrusive thoughts
Or my suppressed emotions

Is it my stupid brain sitting on past
Or my parent's unresolved conflicts

Is it my sense of hopelessness
Or my homeless innerchild's wounds

Is it my overthinking and fear
Or my re-experienced traumas and physical
pains

Is it my weak mindset
Or my unhealed wounds which were denied

Is it my detachment
Or my moments of being scapegoated

Is it my silly lies
Or is it the truths they hide always

Is it my mind living in a bubble
Or is it my shrinked hippocampus not allowing
me to differentiate my past and present

Is it my PCOD
Or is it my PTSD too

Is it all my fault
Or is it the gift I got for holding it strong

Not my fault

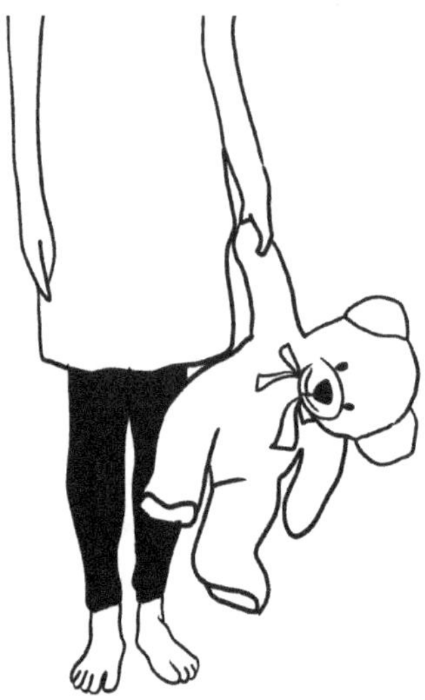

Hey it's not me dwelling on the past
It's the traumas showing up even if I don't want
to

It's not me overthinking
It's my body re-experiencing the trauma even If I
don't want to

Is not my unwillingness to get out of the loop
The only choice given to me is to stay strong
and enjoy the ride even if I don't want to

Outpour

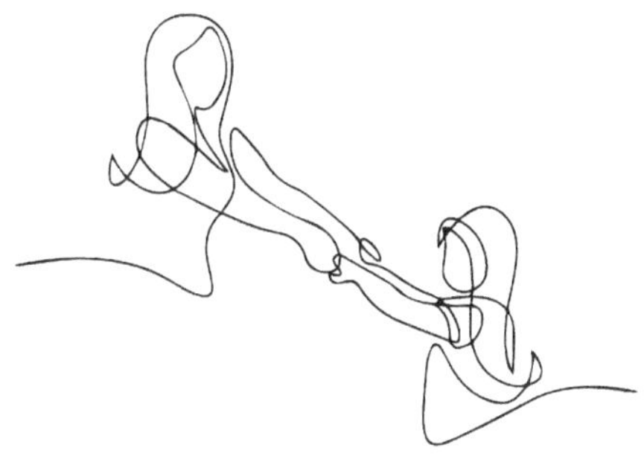

When you said you are not okay,
Did they really check on you or
Did they deny it saying you are weak?

When you cried out of pain
Did they wipe your tears or
Did they leave the place quitely?

When you were facing your hardest battle
Did they cry for you or
Did they laugh at you?

When they needed your help
Did you run to them for help or
Did you stand back?

I know you did everything hoping that they will
be kind to you
But still you went through every hardship alone

Whoever left you at your bad time
Will never think about the good deeds you did

Being a doormat for everyone is a trauma
response
Be there for you before being there for others

Panic attack

It's not just fear
It is the heart palpitations
It is the unexplainable body pains
It is the hunger for breath
It is the growling stomach
It is the stabbing chest pain
It is the uncontrollable shivering
It's when you lose your control without a reason
It's when you can't differentiate whether it is a
panic attack or a heart attack
It's not a choice
It is a disease
Don't ever do self-treatment
Don't ever sit thinking that "it's all in your
head.."
Get out and Seek help
You will find a way out easily!

Questions

Even If my answers were "I don't know"
Her questions for the 5-year-old me turned out to
be the answers for my dysregulated nervous
system

Did people in your home enjoy each other's
company?
How do your dad & mom resolve their
disagreements?
Who made you feel safe?
Who made you feel special?
Can you describe your relationship with your
primary caregivers?
When you were upset who comforted you?
Have you ever felt rejected by your parents?

If the answer made you cry
It's okay
It was not your fault
But let's heal and grow

Resilience

Yes we startle and be on edge always

We disconnect or be reckless anyways

It's okay to go through strange stuffs

Seeking help may be hard but it's worth

Don't feel shameful but feel proud

'Cause you were on survival when others were living

Still you did your best!

Still you've been so kind!

Session

With a bright smile
She said to me, "It's okay, let's fix this"
My teary eyes saw
a tiny ray of hope
Her voice echoed, "It's not your fault"
Two more drops
rolled down to my cheeks
She continued, "Your struggles, emotions and
pain is valid, even if others can't accept it"
My little heart felt light
For the first time when I felt Heard..

Twenty-Nine

I'm still finding myself
Figuring out my purpose
Unclear but not worried
Unsure but not misled

You don't have to settle down
You don't have to finish it off
Life is beautiful when you take it slow
Life is calmer when you do not rush

It's always the journey you have to enjoy
Not the destination.
It's always the moments you have to enjoy
Not the memories.

Uplifting You and Me

My soul wants to float freely

Beyond the skies

Just like an autumn leaf

Colouring joy in everyone's life

Even after falling off

Even after tearing up.

Voice Echoed

Thanks for the hard days
It showed me who really cares

Thanks for the Battles
It gave me the most purest cuddles

Thanks for the isolation
It gave me salvation

Thanks for the pain
It helped me rewire my brain

Thanks for this invisible illness
It gave me a purpose for my existence!

Wellness

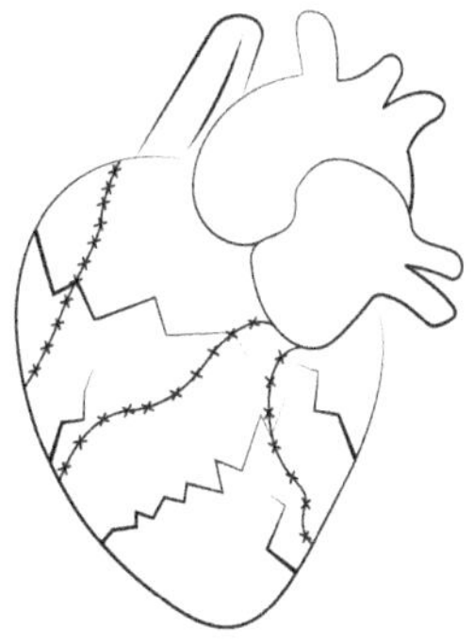

No one will fake illness
Believe them rather than doubting...

No one will cry without pain
Hug them rather than questioning...

No one will seek help without struggles
Save them rather than judging...

You may not have faced it
But that doesn't mean it doesn't exist...

Be kind
Rather than denying...

Xenoglossy

They asked me to speak up
After silencing me with their judgements

They asked me to get over it
After traumatizing me with
Their actions

They asked me to forget
And move on
After gifting me PTSD

It's like asking me to not
Scream After pressing
The unhealed wound...

Y

Why is it always
"People will hurt you
You have to be strong"
Instead of
"People are not always meant to be strong
You shouldn't hurt others"

Why is it always
"Don't speak about it
It's not going to help anyone else"
Instead of
"You don't have to hide anything
It may help you and that matters"

Why is it always
"Don't be so sensitive
That was just a joke"
Instead of
"Don't put anyone down
And expect them to be happy"

Why is it always
"You don't have any problem
I don't see anything"
Instead of
"You may have a problem
Even if I'm not able to see"

Why is it always
"Rest peacefully
You never told"
Instead of
"Take good rest
We heard you!"

Zigzag

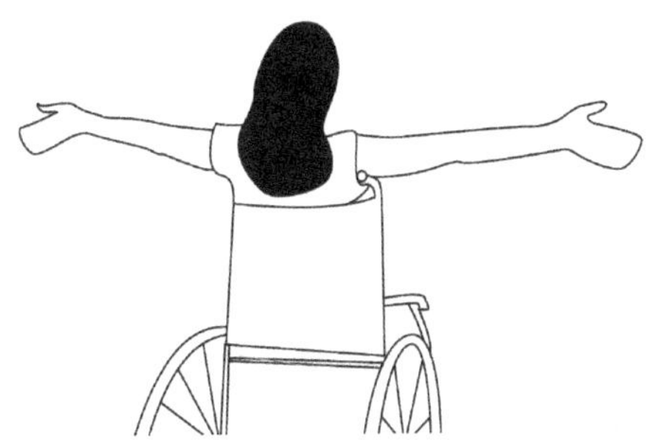

It's a journey through Highs and lows

Let's climb the mountains and valleys

Let's flow with the Wind and the waves

Let's stay together from winter to spring

Let's spend all Nights and days insane

We are here to feel the joy and pain

We are here to live the youth and old age

Let's just breathe the air peacefully

As if it's the first and the last...

Roots

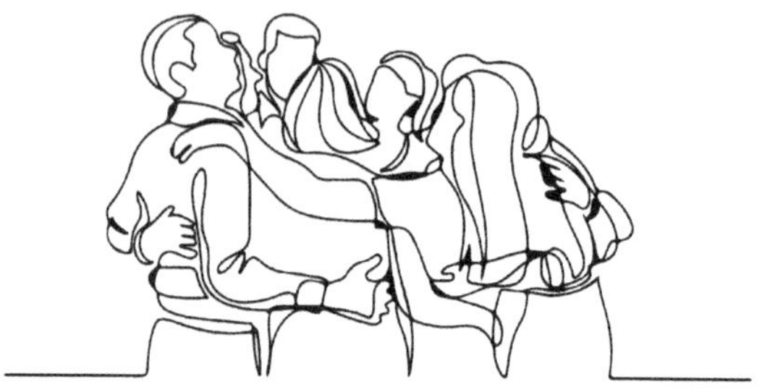

We don't need a religion
To see God

We don't need a colour
To love human

We don't need a size
To admire beauty

We don't need anyone's approval
To live in this world

All we need is a heart full of kindness
For ourselves and for everyone

You have you

Even the darkest night
Seems like dawn
If you are with a good companion.
So who is a good companion?
The one who always whispers
About so many things in silence
The one who wraps your feelings together
The one who loves you
For who you are
The one who never leaves your side
The one who never gives up on you
It's not a person
It's your mind!
Take care of that companion
And never let it lose you!

Rabbit

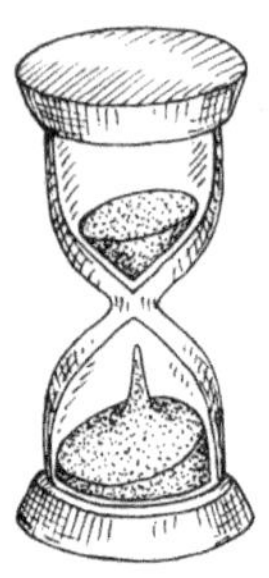

Don't run
Just take a slow walk
Life is not too long
Please don't run

Don't get into a race
There is no prize but it's only the end of life
Moments are right now
Please don't get into a race

Don't rush to the future
Enjoy today, enjoy now
This is the moment you live
Today was yesterday's future
Please don't rush to the future

Don't ever compare
Your purpose of life is unique

Their success won't affect yours
Please don't ever compare

Don't compete
Just enjoy your life to the fullest
As only you got the privilege to live your life
So please don't compete

Healing

I'm still unlearning
To not overthink

I'm still unlearning
To not overshare

I'm still unlearning
To not over care

I'm still unlearning
To not overreact

I'm still relearning
How to be calm

I'm still relearning
How to be peaceful

I'm still relearning
How to be simple

I'm still relearning
How to love

I'm still learning
To love myself more
I'm still learning
To love everyone around

I'm still learning
To be myself

I'm still learning
To let others live their life

I'm still finding myself
I'm still trying to be myself

To just be...
To just be alive and happy!

Alive

Goal is not to be at the top first
Goal is to enjoy the path and the moment

Goal is not to win the race
Goal is to walk out of the race track and lie in
the meadow

Goal is not to hide the pain and show the joy
Goal is to be fine with
Sharing anything without shame

Goal is not to get attention for mental illness
Goal is to bring awareness about the stigmas!!!

Dear mom and dad to be

You don't have to work hard to be a good mom
and dad

You just have to be a happy mom and dad

Your kids don't have to see your efforts

Your kids just have to
See you happy and peaceful

If you are unhappy
Your efforts won't be seen

If you are happy
Your efforts will be their learnings

Unhappy parents
Bring unhappy kids
To an unhappy world
End up in unhappy relationship and unhappy
life...
Please be happy
So you can give a joyful life to your kids

Choice is yours
You can pass down the generational trauma
Or you can be a
Cycle breaker.

Reflections

Piled up cloths
Inside my cupboard
Resembled my messed-up thoughts
hidden and covered

My unfollowed
daily routine
was the same as my repressed memories which
are still Unseen

The Amount of pills I took
like food
was the same as the tears
I shed from my childhood

My uncontrollable
fear and anxiety
was just similar to my own life
living on edge.. losing my own sanity